PAINT BY STICKER

KIDS

DINOSAURS

workman

• NEW YORK •

Copyright © 2020 by Workman Publishing Co., Inc.

ISBN 978-1-5235-1117-4

Design by Ying Cheng

The 10 low-poly images in this book are based on illustrations by Ying Cheng.

Workman books are available at special discounts when purchased in bulk for premiums and sales promotions as well as for fund-raising or educational use. Special editions or book excerpts can also be created to specification. For details, contact the Special Sales Director at the address below or send an email to specialmarkets@workman.com.

Workman Publishing Co., Inc.
225 Varick Street
New York, NY 10014-4381

workman.com

WORKMAN and PAINT BY STICKER are registered trademarks of Workman Publishing Co., Inc.

Printed in China
First printing June 2020

10 9 8 7 6 5 4 3 2 1

HOW TO PAINT BY STICKER

1. PICK YOUR IMAGE. Do you want to sticker the ferocious Tyrannosaurus rex, or the feather-covered velociraptor? It's up to you! Just find the page you want to paint with stickers.

2. FIND YOUR STICKERS. The sticker sheets are in the back of the book. In the top corner of each sheet is an image of a painting page. Find the sticker sheet that goes with the page you want to paint. Both the sticker sheets and the painting pages can be torn out of the book so you don't have to flip back and forth between them.

3. MATCH THE NUMBERS. Each sticker has a number next to it, and each painting page has numbers on it. Match the sticker number with the number on the painting page. Be careful! The stickers aren't removable.

4. WATCH YOUR PAINTING COME TO LIFE! After you've finished your masterpiece, you can frame it, use it as decoration, or give it as a gift.

ARE YOU READY? LET'S START STICKERING!

TYRANNOSAURUS REX

tuh-ran-oh-SORE-us rex

The Tyrannosaurus rex, or T. rex, was one of the largest meat-eating dinosaurs that ever walked the earth. Its jaws were four feet long, with teeth up to 12 inches long! Scientists think that T. rex could eat 500 pounds of meat in just one bite.

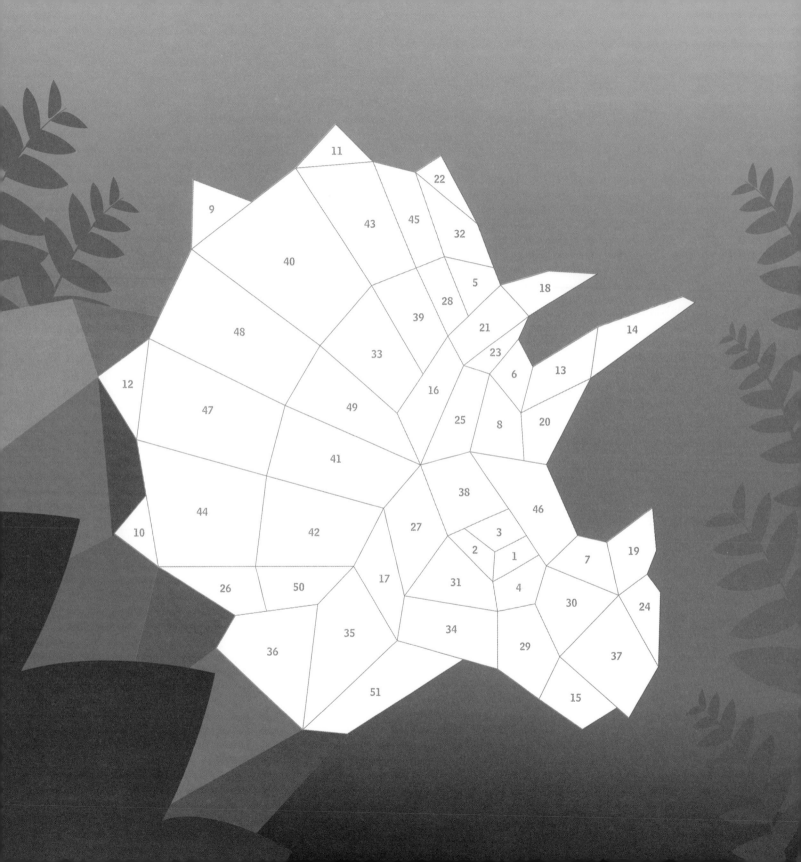

TRICERATOPS
tri-SER-uh-tops

The triceratops had three horns on its face (that's where the "tri" in its name comes from) and a bony plate called a frill growing from its neck. The frill protected it from predators like the T. rex. The triceratops was a plant-eating dinosaur, and had anywhere from 400 to 800 teeth, which it used to chew palm fronds and other tough leaves.

SPINOSAURUS
spine-oh-SORE-us

The spinosaurus was a gigantic meat-eating dinosaur, and the first dinosaur known to have adapted to living in water. It had flat, paddle-like feet, nostrils on top of its head, and a tall spine that stuck out of the water like a shark fin. A deadly predator, spinosaurus ruled the swamps and rivers of northern Africa, eating fish, other dinosaurs, and ancient crocodiles.

ANKYLOSAURUS
an-kuh-loh-SORE-us

The ankylosaurus, a plant-eating dinosaur, was heavily armored, with huge bony plates all over its body that protected it from attacks. Its club-like tail was strong enough to break the bones of any predators—including other dinosaurs.

STEGOSAURUS

steg-oh-SORE-us

The stegosaurus was a slow-moving, plant-eating dinosaur. It had tall plates along its back that helped it attract mates, and it used the long spikes at the tip of its tail to protect itself from predators. Though the stegosaurus was huge, it had a tiny brain, about the same size as a dog's.

BRACHIOSAURUS

brack-ee-oh-SORE-us

The brachiosaurus had a very long neck, a tiny head, and a big appetite! This plant-eating dinosaur munched on the leaves of tall trees, like the ancient ginkgo, and ate between 440 to 880 pounds of food a day.

VELOCIRAPTOR
ve-LAH-suh-rap-tor

The velociraptor was a small dinosaur, about the size of a modern-day turkey. It had hollow bones that helped it move quickly—it could run at speeds of up to 24 miles an hour! Scientists believe that the velociraptor was covered in feathers, just like a bird.

PARASAUROLOPHUS

pair-uh-sore-uh-LOFF-us

The parasaurolophus, a plant-eating dinosaur, could walk upright on two legs as well as down on all fours. Its skull extended upward into a long, curved crest. The crest was hollow and connected to the dinosaur's nasal passages, allowing parasaurolophus to make deep, loud sounds that could travel long distances.

CARNOTAURUS
kar-noh-TORE-us

The carnotaurus was a ferocious meat-eating dinosaur. It had strong thigh muscles that enabled it to run really fast. The two horns above its eyes protected the dinosaur during head-to-head combat with rivals.

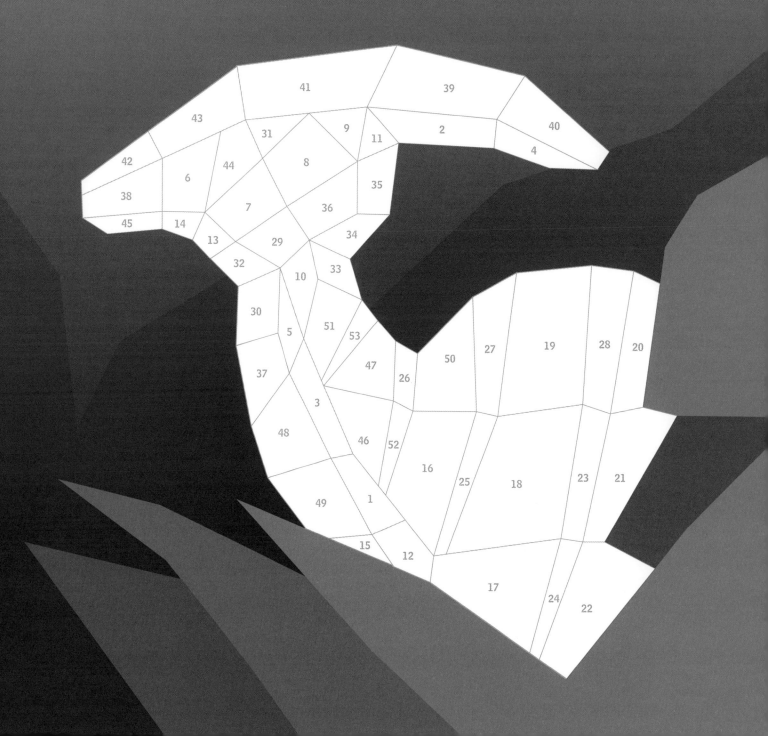

CHARONOSAURUS
ka-rohn-oh-SORE-us

The charonosaurus was a plant-eating dinosaur whose fossil remains were discovered on the banks of the Amur River, also known as the Black Dragon River, in China. Based on the shape of its skull, scientists think that charonosaurus had a long crest at the back of its head, much like parasaurolophus.

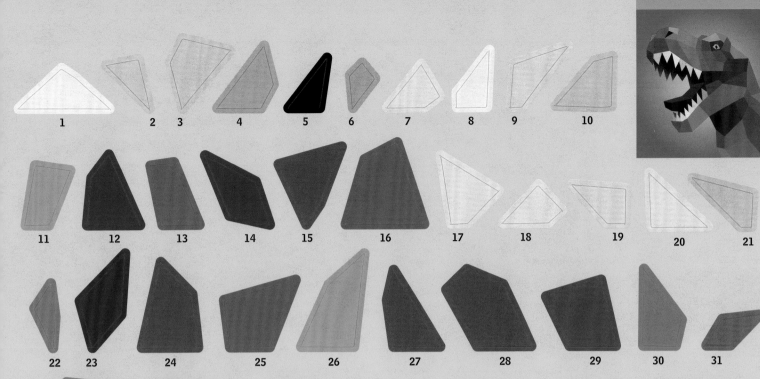

1

2

3

4

5

6

7

8

9

10

11

12

13

14

15

16

17

18

19

20

21

22

23

24

25

26

27

28

29

30

31

32

33

34

35

36

37

38

39

40

41

42

43

44

45

46

47

48

49

50

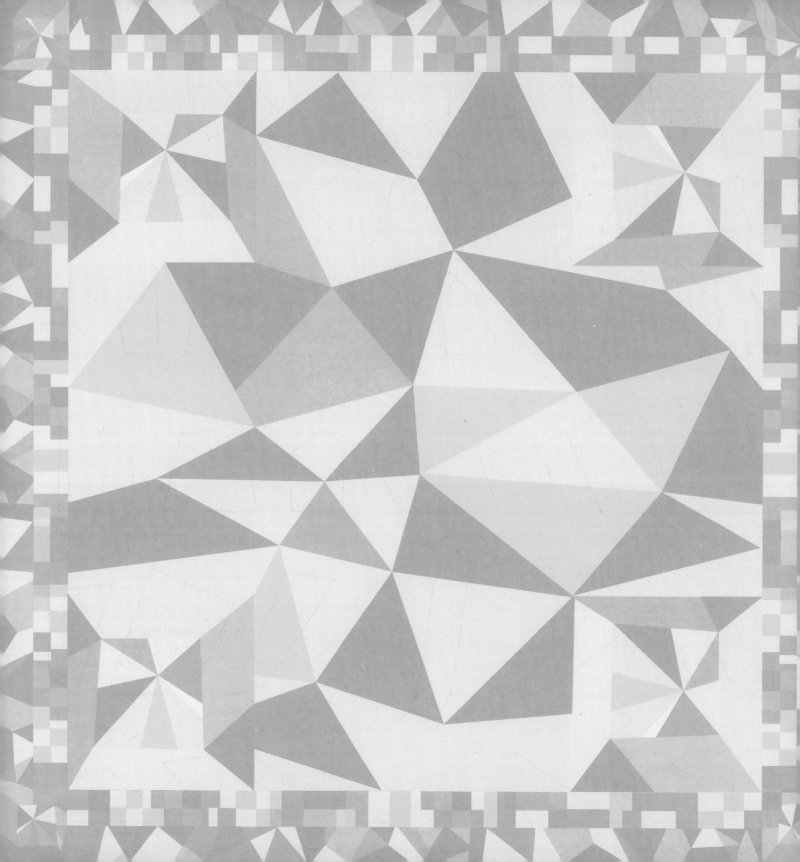

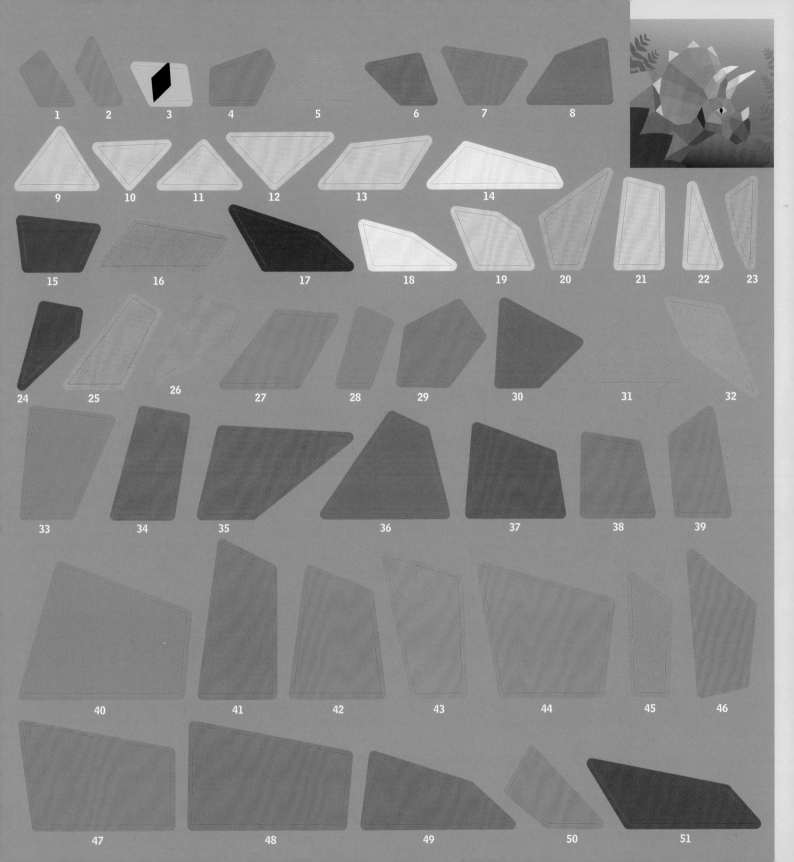

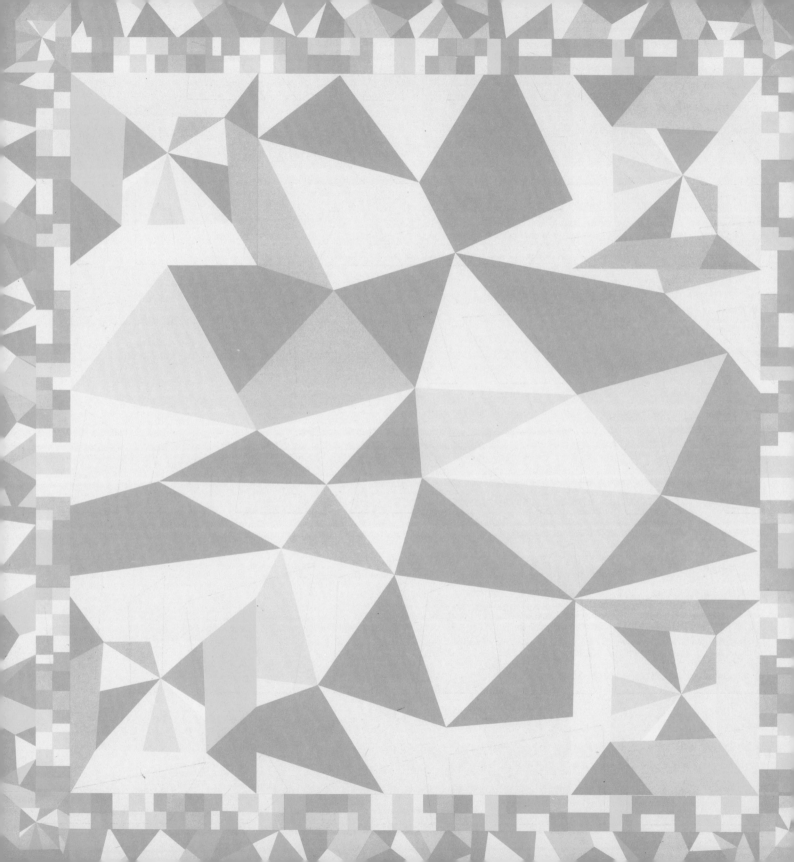

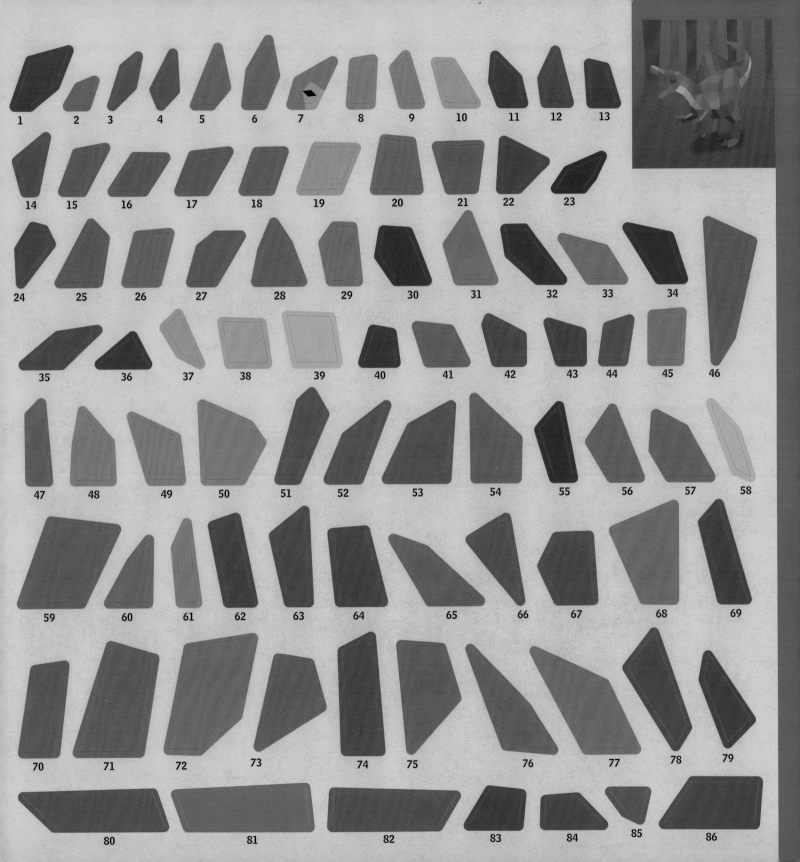

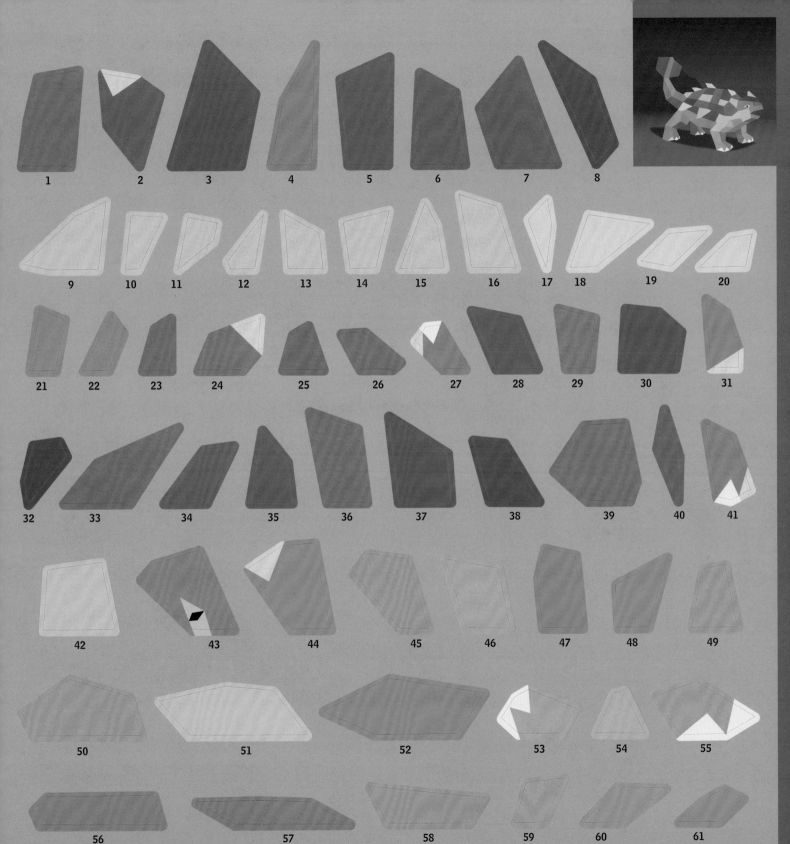

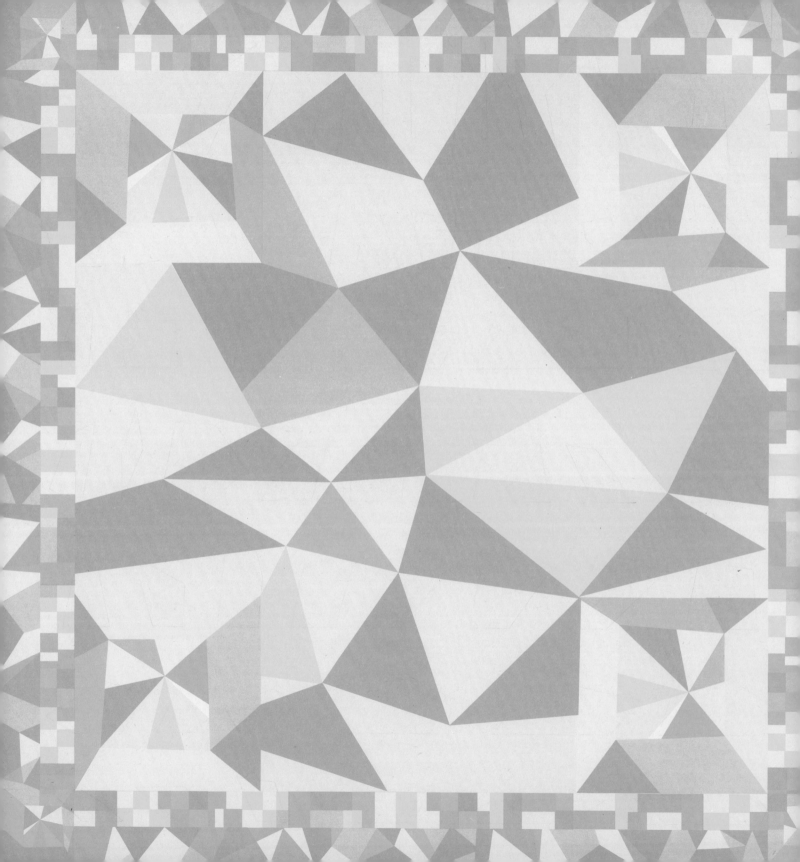

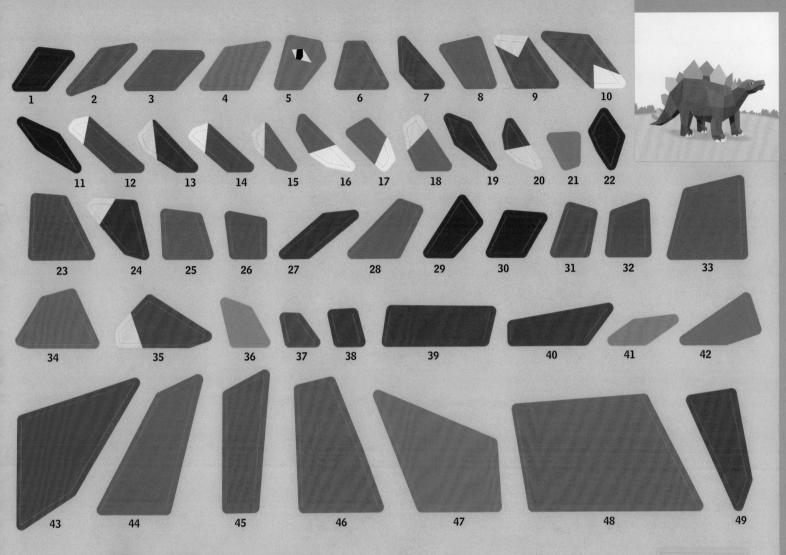

1
2
3
4
5
6
7
8
9
10

11
12
13
14
15
16
17
18
19
20
21
22

23
24
25
26
27
28
29
30
31
32
33

34
35
36
37
38
39
40
41
42

43
44
45
46
47
48
49

50
51
52
53
54
55
56

57
58
59
60
61
62
63
64
65

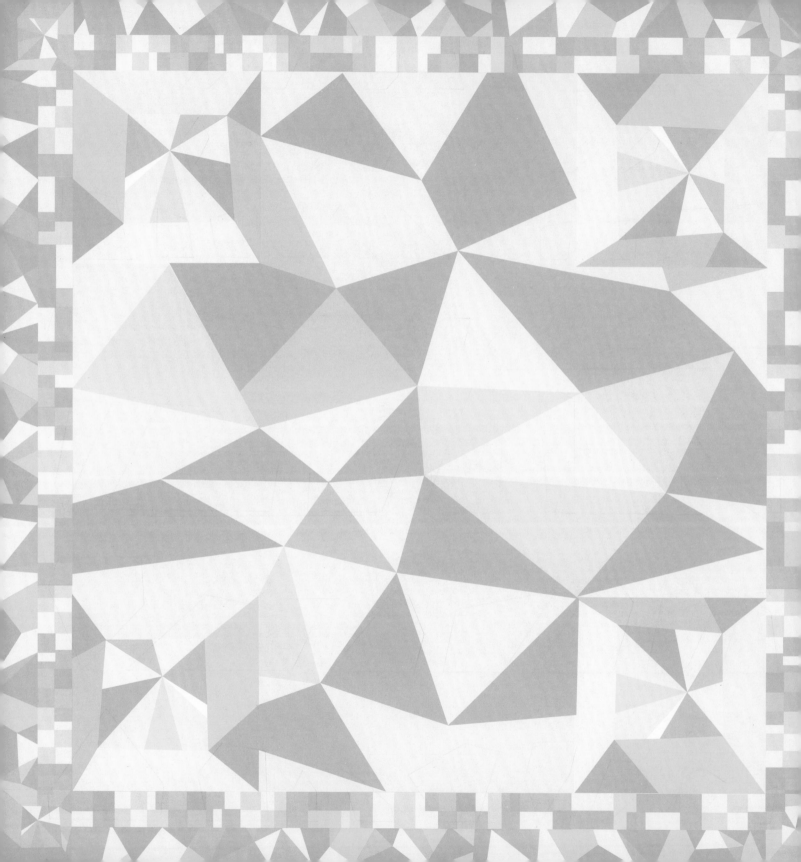

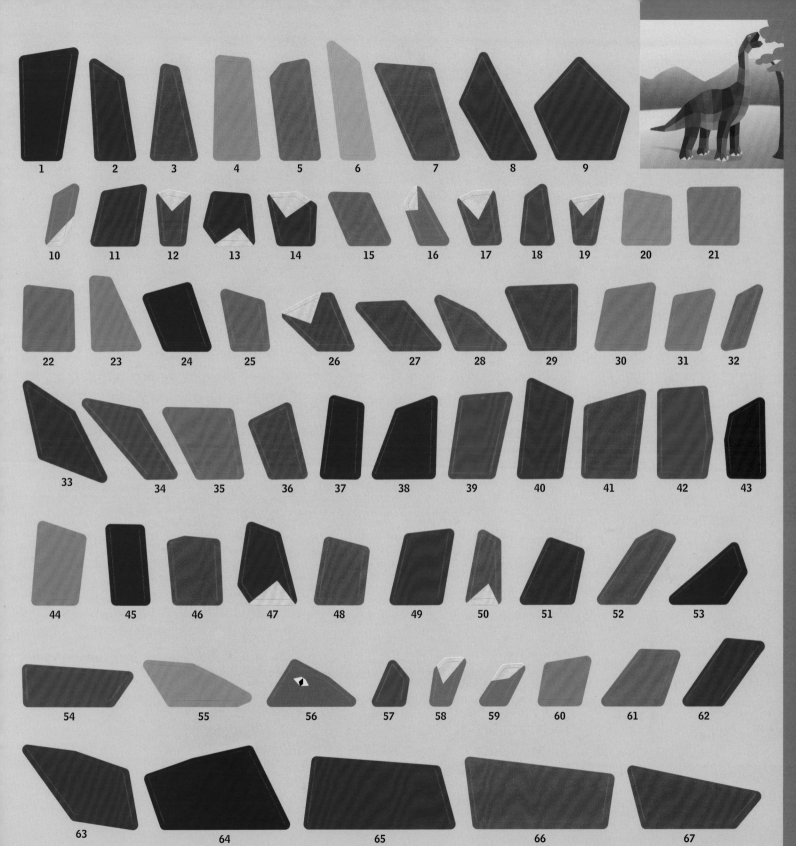

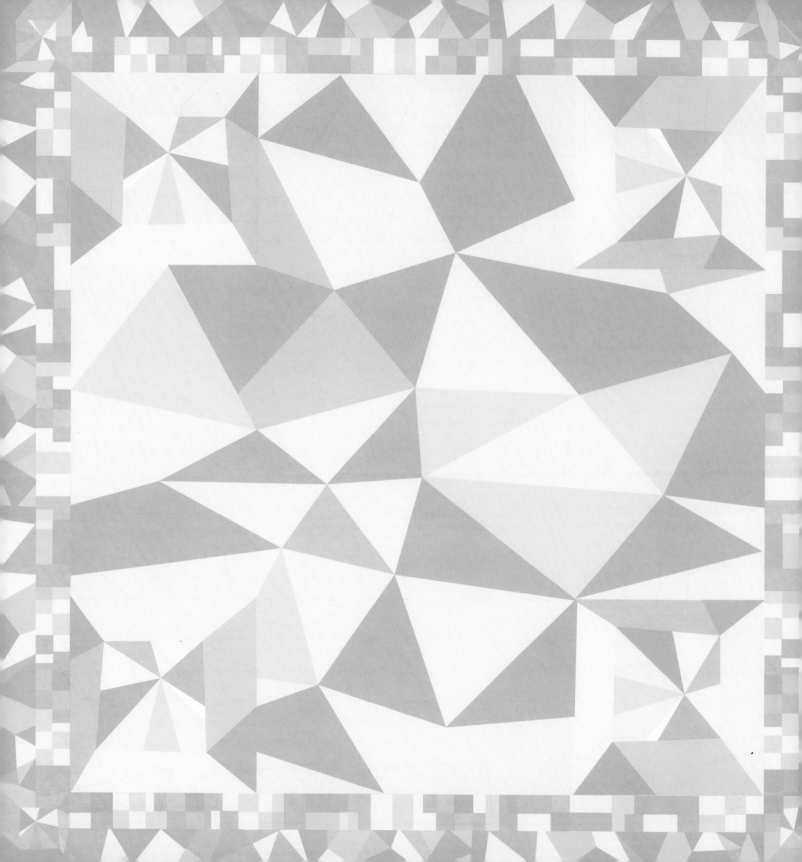

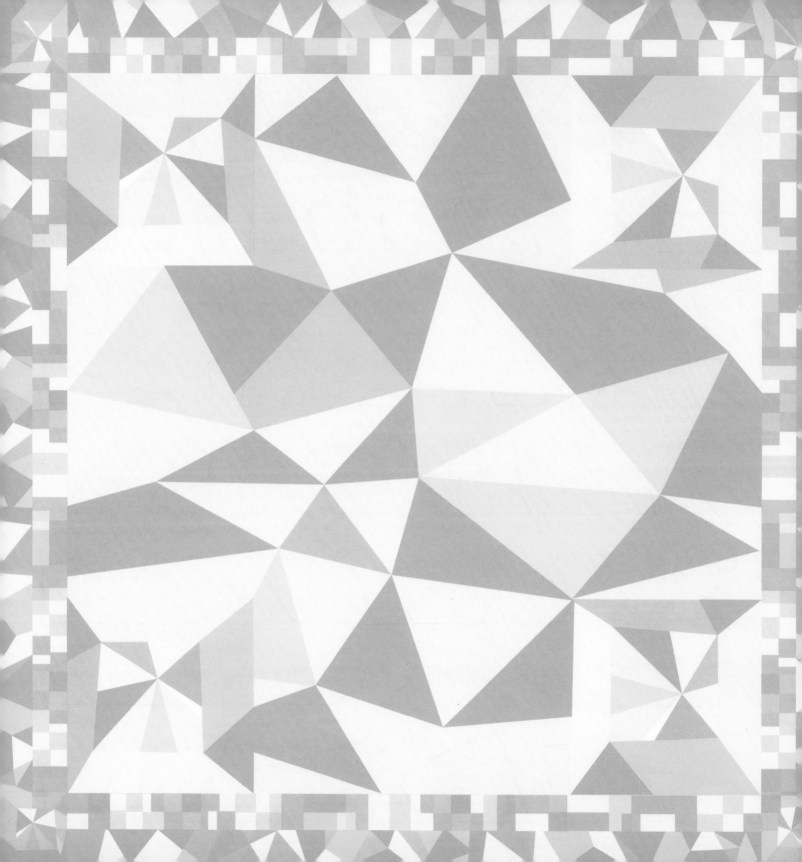

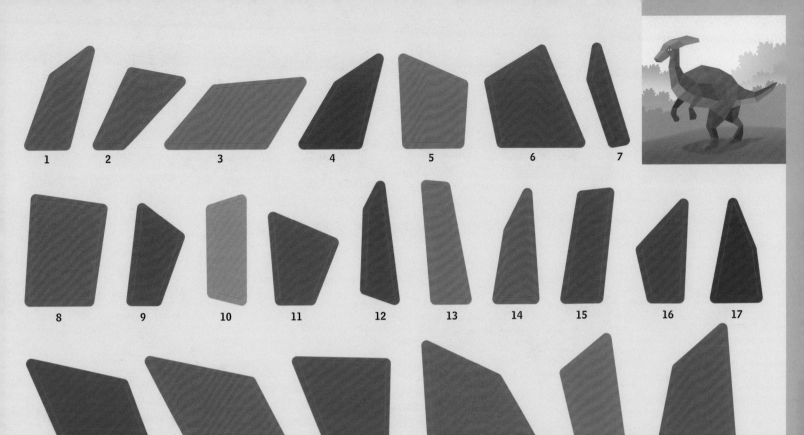

1

2

3

4

5

6

7

8

9

10

11

12

13

14

15

16

17

18

19

20

21

22

23

24

25

26

27

28

29

30

31

32

33

34

35

36

37

38

39

40

41

42

43

44

45

46

47

48

49

50

51

52

53

54

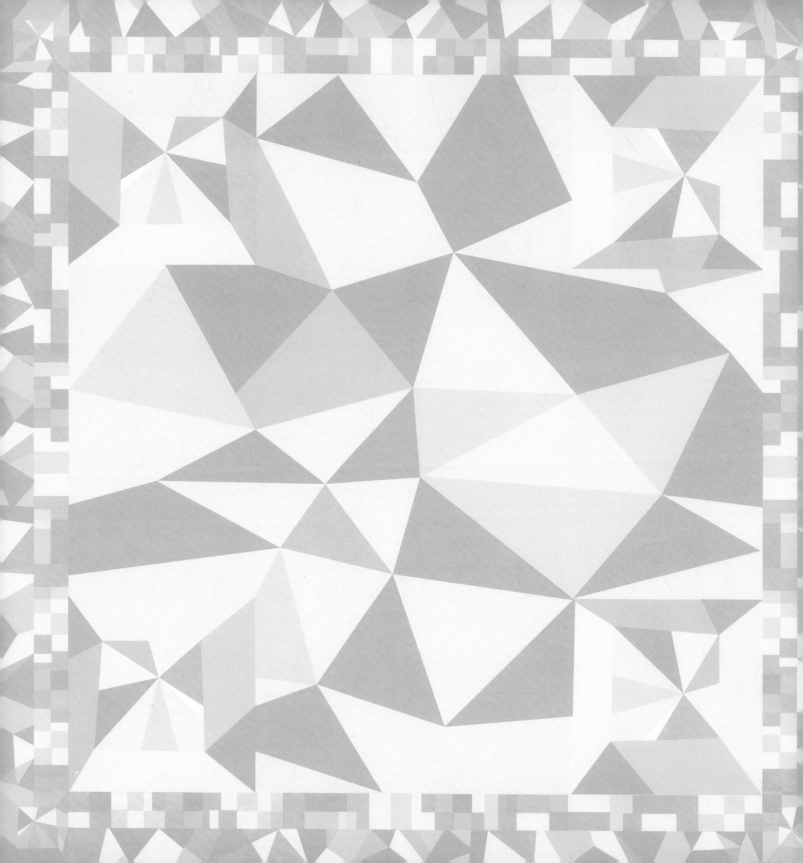

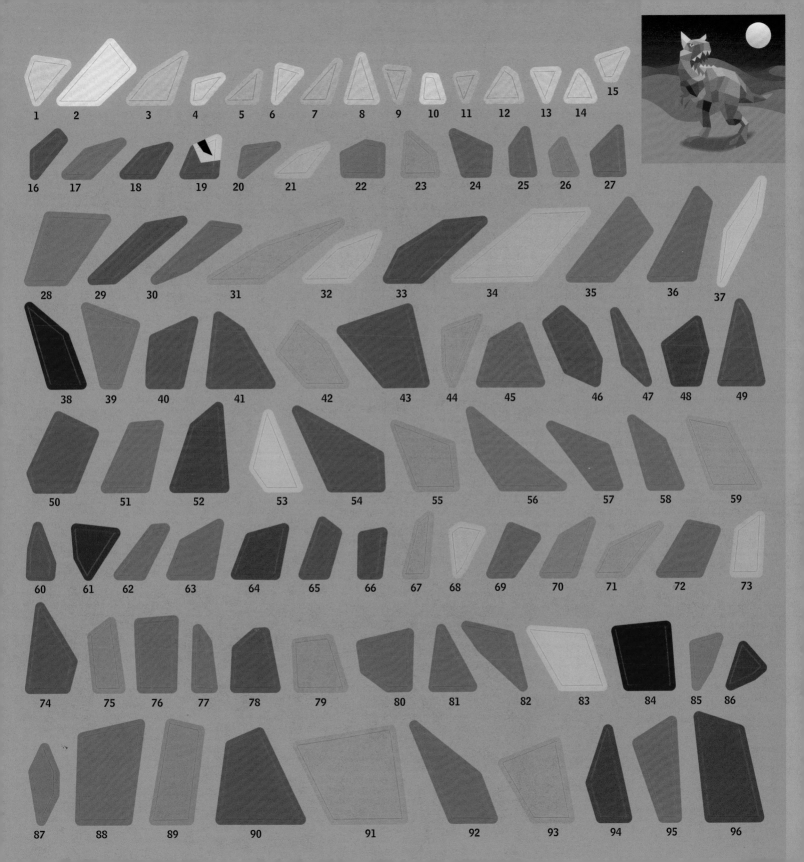

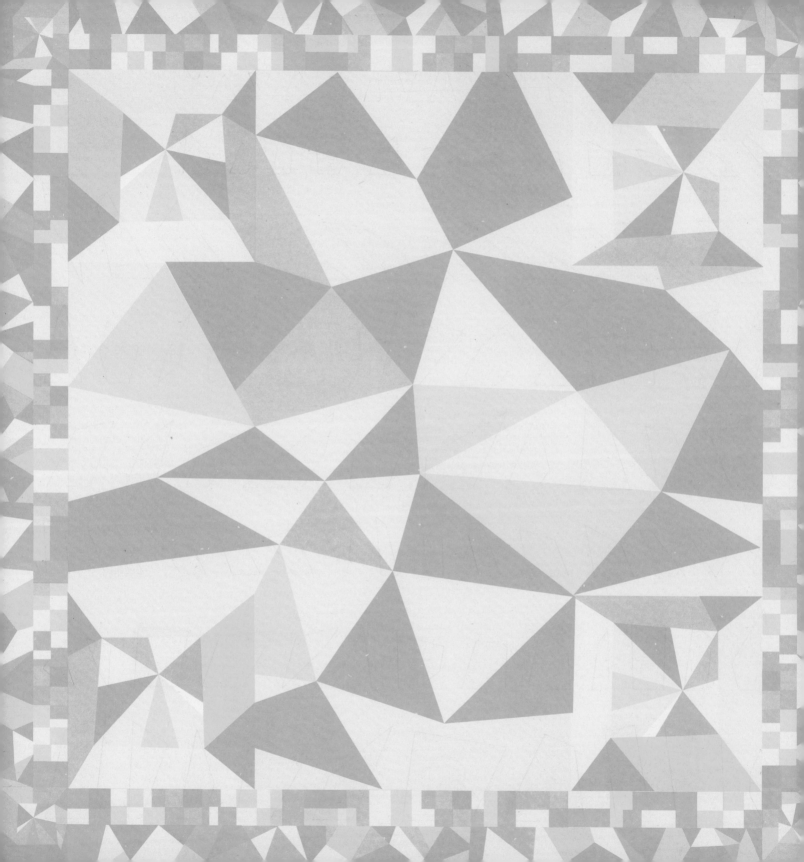

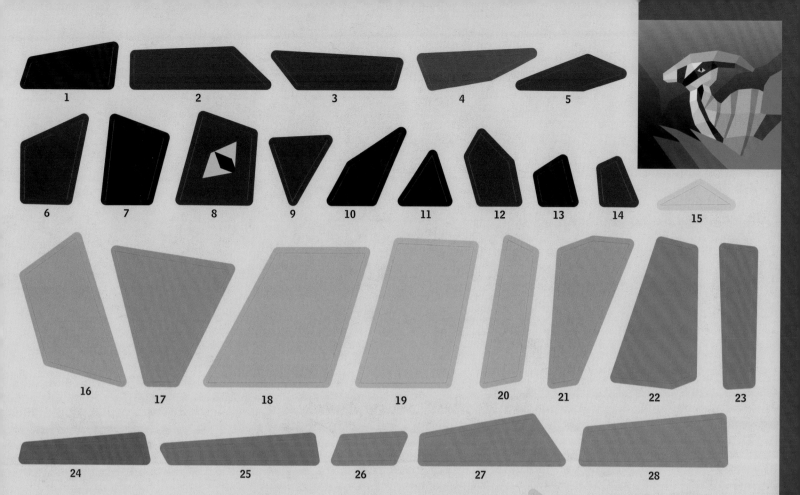

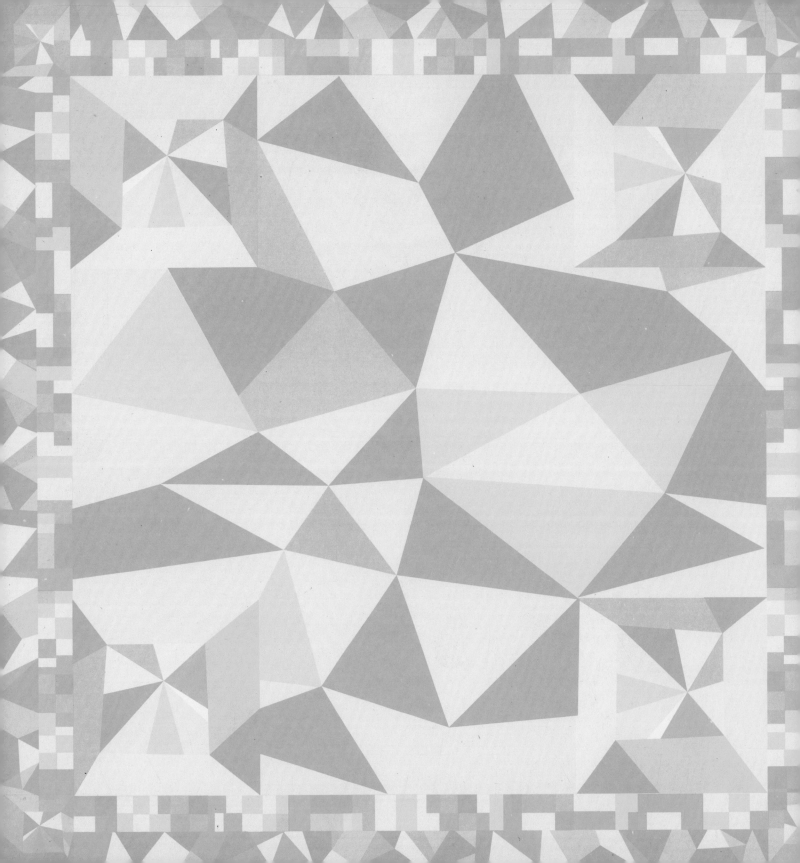